Classified Spelling

Classified Spelling

by
W. J. Leonard, B.A.

SCHOFIELD & SIMS LTD.
HUDDERSFIELD

0 7217 0013 6

Revised and Reset 1972

Second impression 1973

Printed in England by Henry Garnett and Co. Ltd., Rotherham and London.

CONTENTS

PREFACE

The object of this book is to encourage a greater accuracy in spelling by approaching the subject in a systematic and logical manner.

In Part One the chief rules which govern certain classes of words are fully explained and their validity emphasised by application to numerous examples.

Words which are not dependent on any simple rules for their spelling have been classified in Part Two according to their particular letter sequences, for practical experiments have proved that if a child is given a list of words to learn, he will learn the words more readily and with greater permanency if the words have a common sequence of letters than if the words are in a miscellaneous list or even in a list wherein the words have common associations of ideas but divergent letter sequences.

Not only are the words classified according to their spelling, but also they are graded according to their difficulty. Most pages of spelling lists consist of four groups of words of which
(*a*) contains the easier examples suitable for younger or more backward children;
(*b*) contains words of average difficulty;
(*c*) contains more difficult words;
(*d*) is a spread test.

Groups (*a*), (*b*) and (*c*) are in themselves subdivided into four groups of five words. This will provide four daily assignments with a twenty-word test once a week.

W. J. L.

PART ONE: GENERAL RULES

Rules for Forming Plurals

Rule 1

(a) Plurals are regularly formed by adding -s to the singular.

    fire fires   door doors   toe toes

(b) When the word ends in -o, -s, -x, -ch or -sh add -es.

potato	potatoes	box	boxes
loss	losses	march	marches
wish	wishes	lash	lashes

Exceptions. The following add -s only :

    bravo, cockatoo, cuckoo, kangaroo, piano, ratio, salvo, studio, tobacco, two.

    e.g. piano pianos   cuckoo cuckoos

(c) Words ending in -y change the y to ie before adding -s, unless the y is preceded by a vowel (cf. Rule 5, page 15).

misery	miseries	donkey	donkeys
memory	memories	tray	trays
robbery	robberies	quay	quays

(d) Words ending in -f or -fe usually change the f or fe to ve before adding -s.

calf	calves	knife	knives
half	halves	life	lives
wolf	wolves	wife	wives

Exceptions. The following do not change the f in the plural :

    belief, dwarf, chief, proof, roof, grief.

    e.g. chief chiefs   roof roofs

    Note: scarfs or scarves ; hoofs or hooves.

Exercise

Make five columns headed -o, -s, -x, -ch, -sh.
Beneath each make a list of all the nouns that you can find with these endings in the singular form.
Which do you think is the most common of these endings?

Note: The preceding rules also govern Verbs when s or es is required.

e.g. snatch	snatches	annoy	annoys
brush	brushes	confess	confesses

Irregular Plurals

(e) The plurals of some words are the same as the singulars.

    sheep sheep   deer deer   salmon salmon

Can you find any more words like these?

(f) Some words change their spelling in the plural.

mouse	mice	foot	feet	goose	geese
woman	women	man	men	tooth	teeth

Do you know any more words which do this?

(g) The plurals of compound words are formed by making the noun part of the word plural.

    brother-in-law   brothers-in-law
    man-of-war   men-of-war
    court-martial   courts-martial

Make singular and plural lists of any other compound words you can find.

(h) Words taken from foreign languages have unusual plurals.

axis	axes	fungus	fungi
index	indices	terminus	termini
basis	bases	bureau	bureaux
oasis	oases	plateau	plateaux

Do you notice any regularity in the plurals of these words?

Note: child, children; ox, oxen;
        penny, pennies (coins), pence (amount).

Spelling Lists

Nouns

(a)
echoes	flashes	approaches	delays
heroes	leashes	branches	highways
mottoes	splashes	brooches	holidays
potatoes	radishes	couches	journeys
tomatoes	rushes	riches	surveys

(b)
buffaloes	addresses	authorities	leaves
mosquitoes	abscesses	economies	sheaves
tornadoes	buttresses	necessities	shelves
volcanoes	mattresses	memories	thieves
sisters-in-law	successes	tragedies	wharves

Verbs

(a)
catches	lurches	envies	annoys
patches	marches	hurries	enjoys
pitches	parches	occupies	essays
scratches	perches	notifies	buys
watches	preaches	tries	dismays

(b)
astonishes	detaches	oppresses	polishes
extinguishes	launches	possesses	punishes
furnishes	lunches	progresses	splashes
nourishes	quenches	suppresses	washes
refreshes	touches	trespasses	wishes

Exercise

Use these phrases in sentences.

pleasant memories
necessities of life
to practise economics
painful abscesses
tragedies of war
notifies the authorities
suppresses information
extinguishes the fire
occupies the house
lurches against the wall

The 'ie' and 'ei' Rules

Rule 2   i before e except after c when the ie rhymes with dee.

i before e

achieve	grief	niece
belief	handkerchief	piece
besiege	relief	pier
cashier	thief	field
retrieve	siege	fierce

e before i

conceit	perceive	deceive
deceit	receive	ceiling
deceitful	receiver	receipt

Exceptions: seize, weir, weird, either, neither.

Note carefully: The above rule is only true when the ie or ei rhymes with dee.

Look up the pronunciation and notice the spelling of the following words:

ancient	foreign	neighbour
*deficient	forfeit	veil
efficient	*freight	vein
science	height	leisure
eight	*sleight	weight

Exercises

1   Use your dictionary to find the meaning of these * words.
2   Make a list of any other *ie* or *ei* words that you can find.
3   Can you find any more exceptions to Rule 2?

Spelling Lists

(a)			
chief	brief	cried	neigh
belief	friend	fried	their
believe	friendly	lie	receive
grief	thief	tried	weigh
grieve	thieves	tie	vein

(b)			
gradient	fiercely	denied	conceited
retriever	pierce	gaiety	heir
grieving	piercing	variety	receiver
grievous	patience	mischief	skein
town-crier	patient	mischievous	eighth

10

(c)

lieutenant	achievement	deceitful	counterfeit
pierrot	friendliness	eighty	reign
proficient	handkerchief	foreigner	heifer
sieve	science	reindeer	sovereign
unbelievable	conscience	seizure	neighbourhood

(d) *Spread Test*

tied	reins	varieties	proficiency
allies	friendship	eightieth	neighbour
	sufficient	seizing	

Exercise

Use these phrases in sentences.

a piercing shriek	the thief's conscience
a fatal seizure	their great achievements
the efficient lieutenant	a deceitful boy
a wide variety	counterfeit money
an impatient neighbour	a friendly retriever

Dropping the Final 'e'

Rule 3

(a) Words ending in -e drop the e when y or a suffix beginning with a vowel (ed, er, ing, etc.) is added.

stone	stony	inquire	inquiry
acquire	acquired	acquiring	acquisition
combine	combined	combining	combination
declare	declared	declaring	declaration
suppose	supposed	supposing	supposition

(b) Words ending in -e keep the e when a suffix beginning with a consonant is added.

advance	advancement	face	faceless
praise	praiseworthy	hate	hateful

Exceptions:

awful	argument

Note: Some root words are slightly altered before certain suffixes:

hate	hatred	produce	production
persuade	persuasion	reduce	reduction

11

(c) Words ending in ie change the ie to y before adding -ing.

    die   dying   lie   lying   tie   tying

(d) Words ending in -ge or -ce keep the e when adding -ous or -able.

    notice   noticeable   outrage   outrageous

Exceptions: The following words do not follow the general rules :

dye	dyed	dyeing	
singe	singed	singeing	
shoe	shod	shoeing	
agree	agreed	agreeing	agreeable

Spelling Lists

(a)

amusing	aching	compared	amusement
biting	chasing	laced	lovely
coming	riding	raced	freedom
rescuing	sliding	lying	priceless
raging	hiding	noisy	hedgehog

(b)

composition	judging	admiration	agreeable
completed	grudging	relation	ceaseless
confident	ceasing	paused	casement
surging	arranging	refusal	noiseless
arguing	rambling	challenging	statement

(c)

imagination	advertising	encouragement	advantageous
illumination	fatiguing	announcement	changeable
education	valuable	advertisement	courageous
determination	expensive	arrangement	serviceable
examination	adventurous	defenceless	peaceable

(d) *Spread Test*

hoping	inviting	increased	denial
bony	urgent	invitation	vengeance
	angrily	exploration	

Exercise

Use these phrases in sentences.

an expensive education	a fatiguing journey
exciting arguments	serviceable clothes
adventurous exploration	grudging admiration
an urgent invitation	a rambling statement
an advantageous position	angry denials

Doubling the Final Consonant

Rule 4

(a) Words ending in a single consonant (other than w, x or y) preceded by a single vowel, double the consonant when a suffix beginning with a *vowel* is added.

blot	blotted	forget	forgetting
commit	committee	glad	gladden
mad	madden	travel	traveller

Note: allot, allotment ; fulfil, fulfilment, etc.

Exceptions: gas, gases ; parallel, paralleled ;
develop, developed, developing.

(b) In words of more than one syllable (except those ending in l) the final consonant is not usually doubled if the accent is on the first syllable either in the word itself or in the derived word.

consider	considering	refer	reference
differ	difference	ruin	ruinous
market	marketing	scatter	scattered

Note: The final consonant is not doubled when it is preceded by more than one vowel.

claim	claimed	devour	devoured
complain	complaining	esteem	esteemed
conquer	conquering	honour	honourable

Exceptions: cruel, cruelly ;
wool, woollen, woolly.

Exercise

Why is the final consonant not doubled in :

repair	repairing	fear	fearing
honour	honourable	allow	allowing
shelter	sheltering	blunder	blundered ?

Spelling Lists

(a)

blotter	madder	bellowing	neater
hotter	muddy	following	gained
boggy	running	shattered	repeated
foggy	thinnest	sheltered	wooden
wagging	winner	scattering	steamer

(b)

maddening	setting	rendered	concealed
skidded	snapped	recovery	dreaming
barred	trapped	wandering	complained
stirred	trapper	allowance	steaming
gassed	woollen	basketry	explained

(c)

allotted	jarred	allotment	appearance
committed	occurred	consideration	esteemed
permitted	referred	development	threatening
forgetting	levelled	oxen	sleepiness
regretting	travelling	parallelogram	conquered

(d) *Spread Test*

ragged	bigger	tripped	wedding
trigger	flapping	*developing	devouring
	stopped	exceeded	

* Note exception to the rule.

Exercise

Use these phrases in sentences.
>threatened development
>their allotted places
>an esteemed customer
>the five-barred gate
>committed the crime
>conquered his sleepiness
>referred to the dictionary
>permitted to see
>regretting the loss
>the maddened oxen

14

Changing the Final 'y' to 'i' Before a Suffix

Rule 5

(a) Words of more than one syllable ending in -y preceded by a consonant change the y to i when a suffix is added, except when the suffix begins with i.

beauty	beauties	apology	apologies
early	earlier	ready	readiness
forty	fortieth	busy	busily
heavy	heavily	occupy	occupied

(b) The y changes to ie when s is added (that is, the plurals of all words ending in -y preceded by a consonant are spelt with the ending -ies).

Note: (i) Words of one syllable usually keep the -y except before -s, or -d.

dry	dryness	dries	dried
sky	skywards	skies	skied

(ii) The -y is kept when there is a vowel before it.

boy	boys	enjoy	enjoyment
stray	straying	buy	buying

(iii) The -y is kept when the suffix begins with i.

deny	denying	apply	applying
defy	defying	supply	supplying

Exceptions:

day	daily	portray	portrait
gay	gaily	beauty	beauteous
plenty	plenteous	miscellany	miscellaneous
pay	paid	say	said

Exercise

Take the words marked * in the Spelling Lists, below; write the words from which they are derived and use them in sentences.

Spelling Lists

(a)

copied	*babies	*denial	donkeys
cried	*ladies	driest	shyly
defied	flies	earliest	monkeys
denied	skies	*merrily	shyness
replied	sties	*trial	stayed

15

(b)

applied	dairies	*dutiful	applying
supplied	fairies	*librarian	delayed
allied	jealousies	*merciless	*supplying
*prophesied	libraries	prettiness	*obeyed
purified	sentries	*readily	slyest

(c)

countries	*application	alliance	annoying
industries	*industrious	economical	prayer
occupies	*glorious	*tyrannical	*annoyance
*opportunities	mysterious	beautiful	boyish
sympathies	*victorious	plentiful	destroyed

(d) *Spread Test*

buying	straying	frying	*occupation
clumsily	reliable	diaries	dismayed
	everything	friendliness	

Exercise

Use these phrases in sentences.

glorious opportunities   mysterious noises
the victorious general   a plentiful supply
our heartfelt sympathies   reliable sentries
an industrious worker   to make application
economical spending   a tyrannical ruler

The -ful Ending

Rule 6

When -full is added to a word one of the 'l's is dropped.

boast	boastful	mind	mindful
care	careful	rest	restful
peace	peaceful	tear	tearful
hope	hopeful	woe	woeful
joy	joyful	doubt	doubtful
success	successful	thought	thoughtful

Cf. Rule 3b, (page 11).

Note: When the suffix -ly is added to a word ending in -ful there will, of
course, be two 'l's.
    e.g. care, careful, carefully;
       hope, hopeful, hopefully, etc.

Exercise

Make three columns of words by adding -ful, -fully to the following words.

e.g. peace   peaceful   peacefully

truth	*plenty	forget	respect
wonder	fear	mourn	harm
*fancy	*pity	*beauty	hate
deceit	delight	trust	*duty
power	help	wrong	play

*Cf. Rule 5, (page 15).

Note: awe, awful ; skill, skilful.

Spelling Lists

(a)
fearful	careful	needful	fretfully
tearful	hateful	spoonful	truthfully
peaceful	hopeful	helpful	joyfully
restful	spiteful	mindful	painfully
sinful	useful	woeful	

(b)
delightful	eventful	graceful	cheerfully
frightful	fruitful	disgraceful	tactfully
rightful	neglectful	shameful	faithfully
sorrowful	wilful	powerful	wrongfully
trustful	wonderful	wasteful	skilfully

(c)
beautiful	distrustful	awful	sorrowfully
dutiful	doubtful	deceitful	reproachfully
merciful	reproachful	forgetful	successfully
pitiful	thoughtful	fanciful	powerfully
plentiful	skilful	resourceful	rightfully

(d) *Spread Test*
cupful	bashful	boastful	playful
dreadful	mournful	doubtfully	lawful
	distasteful	revengeful	

Exercise

Use these phrases in sentences.

a reproachful look

a dutiful son

disgraceful scenes

a pitiful sight

the rightful heir

mercifully destroyed

a resourceful person

a distrustful nature

the skilful surgeon

a woeful countenance

17

The Apostrophe

Possession

Rule 7

(a) To show *possession* add 's to a word unless the word already ends in -s.
If the word ends in -s. (as most plurals do) add the apostrophe only.
Most proper nouns ending in -s take 's.

Words not ending in -s

boy	The boy's nose
elephant	The elephant's trunk
bird	The bird's head
girl	The girl's face

Words ending in -s

boys	The boys' noses
elephants	The elephants' trunks
birds	The birds' heads
girls	The girls' faces

Note: Generally the apostrophe ' is used only with the names of living things.
Thus we may say "The man's height" but we should say "The height of the pole" rather than "The pole's height".
Nevertheless for periods of time we do use the apostrophe as in :
A day's holiday   In three weeks' time

(b) Possessive pronouns *do not* have an apostrophe.
This is *yours.*
The cat hurt *its* tail.
His hand was cold.

Note very carefully: Do not make the mistake of using an apostrophe with every word that ends in -s.
Remember that the apostrophe ' is only used to show ownership and omission (Cf. Rule 7c, page 19).

Spelling Lists

(a)

The boy's book	The lion's cage
The baby's chair	The dogs' tails
My sisters' hats	The chicken's pen
Your uncles are rich	The women's coats
The king's throne	My father's car

(b) The enemies' plans   Is this yours ?
Your friend's house   An hour's play
The sparrows' nests   This is hers
The foxes' dens   The mice's tails
The children's toys   The camel's hump

(c) My grandfather's watch   That is theirs
The lamb lost its mother   Mr. James's bicycle
The barristers' speeches   In a year's time
The dromedaries' riders   The solicitor's bag
Six weeks' holiday   The rabbit's burrow

Graded sentences for dictation.
1 The cow's horn was broken.
2 She lost her mother's letters.
3 The woman's hat was blown into the road.
4 The donkey's owner was a thief.
5 Charles's dog has lost its collar.
6 Whose shoes are wet ?
7 My aunt's house is in beautiful surroundings.
8 The men's umbrellas were stolen so they borrowed ours.
9 The butterfly's wing was damaged where the boy's finger had touched it.
10 These books are yours; ours were borrowed from Mr. Jones's library.

Exercises
1 Use in sentences the phrases in (a) (b) and (c) above.
2 Write sentences containing the following words in the possessive case: mouse, butcher, neighbour, Iris, rooks, nephew, soldiers, tailor, who, yours.

Omission
(c) The apostrophe ' is also used to show that one or more letters have been missed out of a word. This is particularly noticeable in poetry (i) and in colloquial writing (ii).

(i) Loud roar'd the dreadful thunder.
When royal James obtain'd the crown.
As I came thro' Sandgate.
D'ye ken John Peel at the break o' the day.
She wept and she sigh'd.
The moon rose o'er the pines.
She bow'd her head.
Ne'er another did they see.
'Tis winter now.

19

(ii) "I'll come if I can."
     "It's on the table."
     "We'll be there tomorrow."
     "I'd rather do it now."
     "They daren't touch it."
     "Who's there?"
     "She won't tell anybody."
     "Don't do that."
     "I can't come with you."
     "It's seven o'clock already."

Exercises

1 Write out the above sentences as they would be written without using apostrophes. (That is, all words must be written in full.)
2 Write sentences containing the following words in the possessive case.

man	we	boys	children
rabbit	dogs	Tom	women
cat	grocer	teachers	Mr. Jenkins
swallows	uncle	boxers	policeman
its	hers	theirs	ours

3 Put an apostrophe where necessary in the following sentences.

1 Shell soon bring the books.
2 The monkeys cages are on the far side.
3 Im afraid theyll never win matches.
4 The pigs ear was torn by the thorns.
5 He said that Id taken his pens.
6 The mouses tail was held beneath the cats paw.
7 Ill let you know as soon as hes gone.
8 Im sure mine is better than yours.
9 Hed taken the childrens toys.
10 Im sorry I wasnt able to go with you.
11 "Dont touch that," she cried. "It isnt yours."
12 Hes afraid he lost his fathers knife when he went into the farmers orchard.
13 Now youve seen our garden well come and see yours.
14 Its remarkable how quickly the puppy learnt its name.
15 Were sure that he delivered mothers parcel at three oclock.
16 "He darent say he wouldnt do it," he answered.
17 Toms found his ball but he couldnt find yours.
18 Weve seen the boys mother but he hasnt been home yet.

19 These coats are ours ; yours are on the other pegs.
20 The dogs entrance wasnt noticed until hed jumped up and seized
the doll. There were tears in Annes eyes but Father said that if wed
get the glue from uncles toolshed hed soon mend its broken legs.

REVISION TESTS

(a)	(b)	(c)	(d)
hateful	skywards	esteemed	handkerchief
muddy	changeable	librarian	acquiring
ceiling	complaining	argument	committed
steamer	besiege	woollen	receipt
facing	praising	deceit	appearance
field	deceive	courageous	requirements
readily	thinnest	cashier	seize
neither	noticeable	enjoyment	mysterious
dryness	steadiness	weird	denying
either	persuasion	supposing	outrageous

Double Letters

Rule 8 In words of more than one syllable :

(a) Short vowels are usually followed by double letters or two consonants.

(b) Long vowels are usually followed by single consonants.

căddy	lādy
glŏssy	lōsing
gŭsset	abūsing
hĭdden	hīding
năvvy	nāvy
răgged	rāging
rămmed	frāmed
rŏtten	rōtate
rŭbber	rūby
shăbby	bāby
Stăfford	wāfer
sŭffer	līfeless
wăgging	wāging
wĭnner	rhīnoceros

21

Exceptions:

coming	having	developing	lapel
benefited	tonic	giving	women
living	reference	referee	radish

Exercise

Make a list of further exceptions. How many can you find?

Words with double letters

Double 'l'

(a)

cellar	allow	college	farewell
collar	hollow	collide	thrill
pillar	swallow	folly	gallop
million	seagull	holly	trolley
pillion	skull	jolly	polling

(b)

challenge	allotment	alligator	collision
dwelling	excellent	collector	illuminate
swelling	intelligent	collapse	especially
swollen	billiards	millinery	illustrate
illegal	caterpillar	scullery	usually

(c)

dwell	thrilling	villain	galloping
swallowed	illustration	gallon	actually
	collection	illumination	

Cf. Rules 4a and 4b, (page 13).

control	controlling	deal	dealing
expel	expelling	maul	mauling

Note carefully: till (two 'l's), until (one 'l').

Exercise

Use these phrases in sentences.

The millinery shop	the intelligent girl
the swollen river	the porter's trolley
actually seen	clever illustrations
riding pillion	to see the illuminations
illegal speed	collapse of the wall

22

Double 't'

(a)
battle	better	bitter	attic
cattle	fetter	bitterly	kitten
bottle	letter	glitter	ditty
little	setter	litter	mitten
brittle	settee	twitter	jetty

(b)
butterfly	chatter	kettle	lattice
fluttered	clatter	nettle	pattern
shuttered	shatter	settle	lettuce
spluttered	rattler	mottled	motto
stuttered	pottery	skittle	pattering

(c)
battering	attachment	attempt	buttress
battery	attainment	attentive	cigarette
battlement	settlement	attorney	mattress
battalion	outfitter	attractive	smattering
scattered	petticoat	attitude	matter

(d) *Spread Test*
butter	batter	gutter	attraction
button	mutton	attire	water-butt
putty	attain	cottage	Hottentot
attack	tattoo	bottomless	attaché-case
forgotten	prettily	tattered	typewritten

Cf. Rule 4, (page 13).
 rot, rotted ; sit, sitting ; etc.

Double 'p'

(a)
appeal	upper	kipper	happy
appear	supper	skipper	copper
happen	supple	slippers	poppy
apple	supply	ripple	pepper
apply	oppose	clipping	puppy

(b)
opposing	apparatus	applaud	appearing
opponent	apparel	applause	chopper
oppress	apparent	approach	appearance
suppress	apparently	approval	chopping
supporter	appoint	happened	appetite

23

(c)

appreciate	apprentice	applied	hippopotamus
appreciation	apparition	application	opposition
appointment	appended	disappearance	opportunity
approximate	appendix	disapproval	appetising
approximately	appendicitis	supposition	opposite

Take special care not to confuse the double letters when adding 'dis-' to the following words:

appoint (disappoint)   appear (disappear)
approve (disapprove)

Exercise

Use these phrases in sentences.

approximately right	operation for appendicitis
gaudy apparel	mysterious apparition
complicated apparatus	apprenticed to engineering
an appetising dinner	ungainly hippopotamus
sent on approval	to show his appreciation

Double 'c'

(a)

occupy	acclaim	accost	accent
occupier	accomplish	according	accident
occasion	hiccup	account	accept
occasional	tobacco	accountant	succeed
occur	tobacconist	accuse	access

(b)

buccaneer	accompany	accumulate	accelerate
moccasin	accomplished	accumulator	accessory
occupation	accommodation	accurate	acceptable
occurrence	accordian	accusation	eccentric
succour	unaccountable	accustom	accessible

Double 'n'

(a)

connect	inn	banner	funnel
cranny	inner	manner	kennel
Finn	innings	spanner	tunnel
minnow	linnet	runner	penny
spinney	skinny	tennis	funny

(b)

channel	annually	beginning	cretonne
flannel	anniversary	innocence	tonnage
tyranny	announcer	innocent	cannon
whinny	annoyance	innumerable	cannibal

24

Cf. Rule 4, (page 13).
    sin, sinning ; span, spanning ; etc.

Double 's'

(a)
cress	endless	cross	discuss
dress	essay	loss	massage
press	lesson	gossip	dismiss
depress	message	fuss	passage
confess	messenger	glass	useless

(b)
compasses	passenger	excess	scissors
compassion	countess	doubtless	fossil
expression	duchess	harness	issue
distress	empress	congress	impossible
missile	governess	fortress	pressure

(c)
depression	colossal	massacre	oppressive
procession	dissatisfied	necessity	profession
concussion	gossamer	crevasse	impressive
discussion	embarrassed	harassed	excessive
percussion	pessimist	essential	impression

(d) *Spread Test*
kiss	gusset	glossy	passion
progress	express	mussel	possess
	passport	fussiness	

Exercise

Use these phrases in sentences.

essential details	a pessimistic outlook
colossal statues	deep crevasses
percussion instruments	a terrible massacre
trade depression	suffering from concussion
feeling embarrassed	the harassed farmer

Double 'g'

dagger	giggle	luggage	aggravate
stagger	goggles	rugged	exaggerate
swagger	juggle	shaggy	suggest
trigger	smuggle	straggle	haggard
faggot	wriggle	struggle	toboggan

25

Double 'b'

dabble	gobble	pebble	abbreviate
squabble	wobble	scribble	cabbage
rabble	hobble	robber	rabbit
rubble	hobby	rubber	shrubbery
stubble	flabby	rubbish	stubborn

Double 'm'

command	commit	grammar	jemmy
commence	glimmer	immediate	clammy
commerce	hammer	immense	ammonia
commotion	hammock	recommend	commission
common	hummock	accommodate	Mohammedan

Double 'd'

cuddle	fiddle	bladder	add
huddle	middle	ladder	adder
muddle	riddle	fodder	addle
puddle	giddy	rudder	paddle
sudden	odd	shudder	address

Refer to Rule 4 for doubling the final consonant before suffixes :
e.g.   drag, dragged ; sob, sobbing ;
ram, ramming ; bid, bidding, etc.

Double 'z'

(Very few words are spelt with double 'z' ; the most common are given below.)

drizzle	blizzard	guzzle	nuzzle
buzz	frizzle	fizz	muzzle
nozzle	buzzard	fizzle	dizzy
puzzle	embezzle	dazzle	

Double 'f'

(a)	bluff	muff	coffee	affair
	cuff	muffin	coffin	afford
	fluff	muffle	offend	raffle
	snuff	buffer	offer	traffic
	stuff	duffle	office	effort
(b)	affable	baffling	gruff	inefficient
	affection	chaffinch	gruffness	insufficient
	scaffold	buffalo	scuffle	inoffensive
	daffodil	giraffe	shuffle	suffering
	paraffin	toffee	snuffle	suffocate

26

Most words ending in the -if sound are spelt -ive (as active, native, etc.).
The most common *exceptions* are :
tiff, sniff, stiff, whiff, bailiff, sheriff, tariff, mastiff.

Exercises

1 Use these phrases in sentences.

the nozzle of the hose-pipe	baffling mystery
guzzled his food	an inefficient staff
the buzzard's nest	insufficient material
embezzled the money	snuffled at the door
an affable smile	the tariff rates

2 Make a list of ten words that end in -ive.

Double 'r'

(a)
arrange	arrow	barrier	barren
array	barrow	carrier	purr
arrears	marrow	carrion	carry
arrest	narrow	harrier	terror
arrive	barrel	terrier	carrot

(b)
barrister	irrigate	correction	currency
carriage	irritate	correspond	quarrel
marriage	irritable	corridor	gooseberry
horrible	terrace	erratic	surround
terrible	territory	squirrel	warrior

(c)
terrific	irritation	barricade	embarrass
terrified	occurrence	catarrh	porridge
horrified	Mediterranean	corrugated	ferrule
territorial	quarrelsome	correspondence	interruption
torrential	hurricane	corruption	irregular

(d) *Spread Test*
error	tomorrow	errand	warren
worry	torrent	warrant	gorilla
ferret	merrily	narrate	turret
stirrup	ferrying	furrow	occurring
garrison	surrender	quarry	chirrup

Exercise

Make a list of twenty other words containing -rr-.

27

PART TWO: WORDS NOT DEPENDENT ON ANY GENERAL RULES

Words ending in -ch

(a)
beech (tree)	church	larch	lunch
speech	lurch	march	punch
beseech	porch	parch	bench
leech	scorch	starch	much
screech	torch	search	such

(b)
beach (shore)	coach	flinch	which
peach	poach	pinch	clench
reach	roach	winch	trench
preach	approach	launch	birch
teach	reproach	staunch	branch

(c)
brooch	ostrich	sandwich	touch
chaffinch	couch	crouch	quench
wrench			

Words containing -ch-

achieve	luncheon	bachelor	avalanche
handkerchief	machinery	exchange	entrenchment
mischief	parchment	poacher	purchase
attachment	treachery	preacher	schedule
detachment	archer	teacher	moustache

Words where the 'ch' is pronounced like 'k'

ache	Christ	scheme	monarch
echoes	Christian	school	anarchy
chord	Christmas	scholar	architect
chorus	anchor	schooner	orchestra
choir	chemist	chrominm	chloroform

chronic	stomach	chasm	chiropodist
chronicle	character	chaos	mechanic
lichen	chrysalis	chrysanthemum	

Words spelt with -tch

(a)
batch	patch	ditch	fetch
catch	notch	hitch	sketch
latch	Scotch	itch	stretch
match	scotch	pitch	wretch

(b)
dispatch	twitch	clutch	butcher
hatch	stitch	crutch	kitchen
scratch	switch	Dutch	ratchet
snatch	unstitch	hutch	satchel
thatched	witch	watch	stretcher

Exercise

Use these phrases in sentences.

batch of cakes

cutting a notch

a Scotch mist

scotch the wheel

dispatch the order

hitch in the arrangements

gnat-bites itch

twitching muscles

a ratchet spanner

the thatched cottage

Note: No word begins with 'tch'. Can you find any other words which are spelt with 'tch'?

Words ending in -le

(a)
bottle	mantle	mingle	cradle
cattle	rustle	shingle	handle
settle	startle	table	ankle
little	title	tumble	people
meddle	uncle	axle	rifle

(b)
circle	gamble	fiddle	hustle
icicle	trouble	scribble	turtle
miracle	principle	struggle	sprinkle
muscle	purple	aisle	winkle
treacle	steeple	sickle	twinkle

29

(c)	cycle	cripple	bristle	spectacle
	bicycle	grapple	whistle	disciple
	tricycle	wriggle	wrestle	rectangle
	pinnacle	honeysuckle	prickle	triangle
	obstacle	knuckle	vehicle	wrinkle

(d) *Spread Test*

candle	tickle	gentle	ripple
castle	trample	article.	saddle
	mangle	pineapple	

Exercises

1 Use these phrases in sentences.

a juicy pineapple	a wrinkled forehead
the pinnacle of the tower	the horse-drawn vehicle
obstacle races	shingle on the beach
an amusing spectacle	hanging icicles
the wrestler's muscles	the aisle of the church

2 Refer to Rule 3 and add -ing to :
bottle, meddle, rustle, startle, mingle,
tumble, gamble, scribble, cycle, trample.

3 Add -y to :
shingle, treacle, prickle, bristle, gentle.

Words ending in -al

(a)	fatal	capital	medal	animal
	metal	mortal	pedal	rural
	petal	postal	rival	signal
	total	comical	spiral	loyal
	mental	local	rascal	royal

(b)	medical	arrival	denial	external
	musical	interval	material	internal
	poetical	revival	special	original
	tropical	survival	general	national
	hospital	manual	several	funeral

(c)	accidental	hysterical	neutral	cathedral
	crystal	technical	diagonal	*principal
	horizontal	electrical	educational	rehearsal
	ornamental	typical	mechanical	residential
	sentimental	practical	municipal	terminal

(d) *Spread Test*

sandal	central	usual	casual
gradual	admiral	marshal	decimal
critical	recital	regional	corporal
carnival	historical	colonial	cylindrical
trial	additional	dental	confidential

Exercise

1 Show, in sentences, the difference in meaning between 'principal', the word marked * in (c) at the bottom of page 30 and the word 'principle'.

2 Refer to Rule 4 and add -ed to :
    total, pedal, signal, rival, metal
Use each of the words you have formed in sentences.

Words ending in -el

(a)
model	camel	bevel	angel
jewel	kernel (nut)	level	chapel
towel	panel	novel	laurel
trowel	label	revel	parcel
vowel	rebel	travel	vessel

(b)
chisel	sentinel	caramel	lintel
tassel	shovel	cockerel	cancel
tinsel	shrapnel	mackerel	enamel
duel	channel	quarrel	shrivel
fuel	colonel	scoundrel	spaniel

Exercise

Use these phrases in sentences :
    tinsel decorations
    the colonel's sword
    the kernel of the nut
    a crowing cockerel
    bursting shrapnel
    sticky caramels
    a wicked scoundrel
    challenged to a duel
    the lively spaniel
    cancel the arrangements

REVISION TESTS

(a)	(b)	(c)	(d)
heroes	snatches	wrongfully	plentiful
trays	addresses	quenches	encroaches
hurries	dwarfs	delightful	respectfully
children	geese	nourishes	mosquitoes
I'll	fanciful	progresses	possesses
dresses	they'll	volcanoes	yours
splashes	potatoes	sons-in-law	apprentices
fearfully	powerfully	hers	brothers-in-law
scornful	wharves	chiefs	distinguishes
leaves	radishes	necessities	extinguishes

Words ending in -ence or -ent

(a)	absence	absent	defence	accident

(a)	absence	absent	defence	accident
	difference	different	licence (noun)	prevent
	evidence	evident	pence	client
	silence	silent	presence	torrent
	violence	violent	pretence	present
(b)	benevolence	benevolent	confidence	confident
	innocence	innocent	dependence	frequent
	impudence	impudent	excellence	excellent
	obedience	obedient	residence	insolent
	prudence	prudent	insolence	dependent (adj.)
(c)	convenient	audience	adjacent	convenience
	correspondent	circumference	inconvenient	correspondence
	impertinent	conscience	diligent	impertinence
	intelligent	consequence	magnificent	intelligence
	prominent	interference	efficient	prominence
(d)	*Spread Test*			
	sentence	parent	student	incident
	negligence	reference	apparent	science
	influence	resident	commence	experience
	opponent	existence	ascent	occurrence
	ancient	negligent	descent	sufficient

Note: (i) -ment is a common ending to many words.

(ii) Few words end in -ense. The most common are :

dense	immense	license (verb)	recompense
expense	incense	nonsense	sense
	suspense	tense	

Words ending in -ance or -ant

(a)
importance	important	tenant	advance
instance	instant	elephant	clearance
defiance	defiant	merchant	allowance
assistance	assistant	peasant	substance
attendance	attendant	pleasant	balance

(b)
vacancy	vacant	annoyance	appearance
constancy	constant	finance	appliance
elegance	elegant	insurance	inhabitant
abundance	abundant	riddance	remnant
fragrance	fragrant	circumstance	stagnant

(c)
extravagance	extravagant	accountant	acquaintance
ignorance	ignorant	descendant	vengeance
disappearance	reluctant	sergeant	perseverance
countenance	lieutenant	restaurant	nuisance
conveyance	significant	indignant	hindrance

(d) *Spread Test*
servant	performance	grievance	ambulance
reliance	resemblance	assailant	tyrant
	remembrance	disturbance	

Exercise

Use these phrases in sentences.

remnant sales	his constant companion
fragrant flower	vowing vengeance
a significant glance	reckless extravagance
a disagreeable countenance	a striking resemblance
elegant clothes	an old-fashioned conveyance

Words ending in -tion

(a)
intention	nation	addition	creation
invention	ration	ambition	situation
mention	station	condition	education
fiction	correction	auction	action
friction	direction	question	operation

(b)
satisfaction	conversation	consolation	exception
subtraction	coronation	examination	competition
transaction	destination	exclamation	description
construction	foundation	population	function
destruction	illustration	reputation	reception

33

(c)	abdication	ammunition	assassination	celebration
	application	exhibition	restoration	consumption
	communication	recognition	appreciation	description
	multiplication	execution	association	suggestion
	qualification	exhaustion	recitation	restriction

(d) *Spread Test*

	fraction	position	promotion	preparation
	motion	suction	regulation	introduction
	caution	imitation	corporation	distribution
	donation	exertion	prevention	persecution
	solution	junction	opposition	congregation

Exercise

Write down the words from which these words are derived:

invention	correction	education	construction
description	destruction	examination	exclamation

Words ending in -sion

(-tion is the more common ending. The most common words ending in -sion are listed below.)

(a)	admission	expansion	collision	conclusion
	commission	mansion	division	confusion
	mission	decision	provision	invasion
	permission	explosion	revision	occasion
	passion	extension	vision	persuasion

(b)	concussion	depression	exclusion	compulsion
	discussion	oppression	illusion	expulsion
	expression	procession	intrusion	session
	impression	profession	television	omission
	submission	succession	transfusion	transmission

Other words ending in the -shon sound

Note: -tion and -sion are by far the most common of the endings pronounced -shon.

Be careful of the spelling of these words so as not to confuse their endings:

fashion	musician	Russian	complexion
cushion	physician	Prussian	inflexion
	freshen	ocean	

Exercises

1 Write out the following words adding the correct 'shon' ending (modify the spelling where necessary):

confess	exclude	connect	omit
conduct	explore	electric	attend
	obstruct	destroy	

2 Use these phrases in sentences.

earning commission	building an extension
needed much persuasion	a striking impression
an air of submission	to the exclusion of everything
ill-mannered intrusion	under compulsion
omission of the word	the transmission of sound

Words ending in -er

(This is the most common of this type of ending.)

(a)	baker	bitter	alter (change)	draper
	miner	hammer	chapter	boarder
	prayer	manner	disorder	leather
	spider	pepper	farmer	saucer
	tower	terrier	register	weather
(b)	answer	announcer	employer	conquer
	cauliflower	character	explorer	foreigner
	coroner	cylinder	gardener	slaughter
	lawyer	minister	passenger	soldier
	*November	remember	traveller	surrender

Words ending in -ar

(There are very few words with this ending. The most common are listed below).

cellar	circular	guitar	similar
collar	particular	calendar	burglar
pillar	popular	caterpillar	familiar
beggar	regular	cigar	scholar
grammar	peculiar	vinegar	irregular

Learn these words ending in -ar very carefully so that you will not confuse them with the words ending in -er.

Exercise

'er' is a very common ending. Make a list of twenty other words you know which end in -er.

*Note: All proper nouns — that is, names of people, countries, etc. — are spelt with a capital letter.

Words ending in -or

(a)
manor	door	error	sailor
mayor	floor	terror	tailor
minor	moor	mirror	traitor
major	poor	junior	motor
razor	visitor	senior	tutor

(b)
accumulator	exterior	author	captor
reactor	inferior	debtor	corridor
conductor	interior	doctor	creator
conqueror	superior	solicitor	instructor
governor	sculptor	survivor	radiator

Words ending in -our

armour	flavour	devour	behaviour
colour	honour	harbour	detour
favour	humour	odour	dishonour
labour	valour	rumour	endeavour
vigour	parlour	vapour	splendour

The following words drop the 'u' in some words derived from them :

honour	honorary	*Note:* honourable
humour	humorist	humorous
labour	laborious	laboratory
odour	odorous	
vapour	vaporize	
vigour	vigorous	

Exercise

Use these phrases in sentences.
inferior workmanship
vigorous blows
dishonoured his family
the only survivor
the soldier's valour
endeavouring to swim

Words ending in -able

(a)
able	cable	lovable	constable
fable	gable	remarkable	reliable
sable	disable	suitable	miserable
stable	usable	valuable	reasonable
table	durable	vegetable	liable

(b)

advisable	changeable	honourable	creditable
dependable	noticeable	incurable	profitable
perishable	agreeable	inflammable	desirable
questionable	rateable	justifiable	respectable
unbelievable	unrecognizable	unmistakable	pliable

Words ending in -ible

(Few words end in -ible. The most common are given here.)

audible	edible	invisible	contemptible
incredible	horrible	legible	invincible
crucible	indelible	possible	plausible
digestible	infallible	responsible	terrible
divisible	visible	sensible	forcible

Note: All these words drop the -le when the common suffix -ly is added :
miserable, miserably ; horrible, horribly.

Exercise

Use these phrases in sentences.
barely audible
an incredible story
edible fungus
The Invincible Armada
perishable goods
creditable results
an unrecognizable photograph
a justifiable mistake
a forcible argument
a beautiful sable coat

Words with silent letters

Silent 'g'

sign	consignment	ensign	gnarled
signpost	neigh	feign	gnash
design	neighbour	foreigner	gnat
designer	sleigh	sovereign	gnaw
resign	diaphragm	phlegm	gnome

Silent 'b'

bomb	crumb	climb	debt
bomber	dumb	climber	debtor
comb	numb	plumber	doubt
beach-comber	thumb	plumb-line	doubtful
tomb	limb	door-jamb	lamb

Silent 'k'

knack	knife	knapsack	knob
knave	knight	knead	knot
knee	knit	knell	knock
kneel	knitting	know	knocker
knelt	knoll	knowledge	knuckle

Silent 'w'

wrangle	wretch	wrist	wreck
wrap	wriggle	write	wreckage
wrathful	wrench	writing	wheelwright
wreath	wrestle	wring	wry
wren	wrong	wrinkle	awry

Silent 'p'

psalm	pneumonia	receipt	psychology
pneumatic	consumption	pseudonym	ptarmigan

Note: The silent 'ch' in yacht (pronounced yot).

Words beginning with dis-

(a)
dismay	disgust	discuss	disable
display	*distrust	dismiss	dismal
displace	distract	distress	*disagree
disarm	district	*dislike	disease
disobey	distinct	disturb	*displease

(b)
discover	discount	disturbing	disqualify
*disorder	*dismount	disturbance	*disrespectful
distemper	disclose	discharge	dismantle
disaster	distraction	*dishonest	disgrace
disastrous	disguise	disinfect	disprove

(c)
*disagreeable	*disadvantage	*disability	*dissatisfied
*discreditable	*disarrange	*disappointment	dissipated
discipline	discontinue	discoloured	dissent
disfigurement	disentangle	disillusion	dissolve
distribute	disobedience	distinguish	dissect

(d) *Spread Test*
dispose	distance	disfavour	disposition
dispute	disperse	discomfort	disobedient
dispel	disfigure	disconnect	dispensary
distil	disregard	discontent	disgraceful
distend	disciple	disbelieve	disapproval

Exercises

1 Make a list of the words marked * and opposite them write the words from which they are derived.
2 Use each of these words in sentences.

Words beginning with des-

descend	desert	desolate	destination
descendant	deserter	despair	destiny
descent	deserve	desperate	destroy
describe	design	despise	destruction
description	desire	despondent	despatch or dispatch

Notice these words cannot be split like most of the words which begin with dis-.
e.g. We can use the words disfavour and favour, but although we use the word descend, there is no word 'cend'.

Exercises

1 From the words beginning with dis-, on page 39, make a list of those which you can split into two parts.

Note: Dis- is the more common beginning. Few words begin with des-. The most common of these are listed on page 39 and should be learned carefully to avoid confusion.

2 Use these phrases in sentences.

a descendant of royalty
desire for power
desolate moorlands
a deserving cause
sharp descents
in desperate need
an unknown destination
a despondent attitude
an excellent description
wilful destruction

REVISION TESTS

(a)	(b)	(c)	(d)
sign	inhabitant	dishonour	yacht
allowance	extension	physician	omission
admission	debtor	convenience	vigorous
visitor	vegetable	knuckle	suggestion
collar	musician	inflammable	complexion
evident	survivor	competition	digestible
reliable	difference	peculiar	wrestle
intention	knowledge	submission	irregular
cushion	conversation	gnome	perseverance
thumb	vinegar	abundance	correspondent

Words containing -au-

(a)			
applause	saucer	aunt	auction
because	saucepan	haunt	fault
cause	fraud	taunt	August
pause	caught	caution	laurel
laugh	taught	cautious	author

40

(b)

gaunt	autumn	Austria	assault
haunch	gauge	Australia	gauze
launch	precaution	sausage	auctioneer
laundry	taut (tight)	audit	overhaul
saunter	undaunted	naughty	cauldron

(c)

audacious	draught	chauffeur	daughter
authority	laughter	gauntlet	cauliflower
autograph	exhaustion	beautiful	haughty
automatic	somersault	bureau	restaurant
automobile	tarpaulin	portmanteau	slaughter

(d) *Spread Test*

daub	haul	sauce	maul
applaud	astronaut	staunch	paunch
laughable	dauntless	augment	auburn
haulage	authorize	cautiously	haughtily
exhaust	laundress	fraudulent	naughtiness

Exercise

Can you find any more words which contain 'au'?

Words containing -ua-

(a)

quack	quarry	equal	gradual
quaint	quaver	unequal	persuade
quaintness	squall	equality	usual
qualify	square	quake	truant
quality	January	quarter	language

(b)

equator	actually	annual	acquainted
equation	estuary	annually	squabble
quantity	situated	continual	persuasion
quarrel	situation	gradually	squander
quarrelled	manual	punctual	valuable

(c)

aquarium	guard	guarantee	acquaintance
qualification	blackguard	*February	punctuality
quarrelsome	coastguard	squalid	continually
*quay	guardian	persuasively	*victuals
squadron	mudguard	unusually	individual

Notice that q is always followed by u :

queer	quiet	question	*physique
quick	quilt	frequent	require

Pay particular attention to the pronunciation of the words marked *.

Exercise

Use these phrases in sentences.

living in squalid surroundings	a quaint old town
applying for a situation	the Thames Estuary
squandered his fortune	sailors on the quay
a thorough blackguard	talked persuasively
guaranteed for six months	cold victuals

Words spelt with gh

Where the -gh- is silent

(a)

blight	high	fight	bough
bright	nigh	flight	though
night	sigh	might	plough
right	thigh	plight	through
sight	taught	tight	dough

(b)

bought	caught	neigh	frightful
fought	daughter	weigh	borough
nought	haughty	weight	nightingale
sought	naughty	eight	thorough
thoughtful	slaughter	freight	wheelwright

Note: Words derived from the above are also spelt with the silent -gh-.

bright	brightly	brightness
light	lightning	twilight
night	nightmare	nightdress
		etc.

Where the 'gh' is pronounced as 'f'

cough	enough	rough	tough
laugh	laughing	laughter	trough
	draught	draughty	

Where the 'gh' is pronounced as 'g'

ghost	aghast	gherkin	ghastliness
ghostly	ghastly	ghetto	ghoul

Exercise

Make a list of any other 'gh' words that you can find and classify them as above.

Words spelt with ph

Words beginning with ph-

phase	Pharisee	phantom	physicist
phrase	phlegm	pheasant	physical
	physician	physique	

Words ending in -ph

nymph	cenotaph	graph	paragraph
triumph	epitaph	autograph	telegraph
	photograph		

Words containing -ph-

(a)
elephant	camphor	emphatic	microphone
graphic	camphorated	emphasise	prophet
orphan	nephew	geography	telephone
orphanage	siphon	sulphur	prophecy
semaphore	typhoon	sulphurous	alphabet

(b)
sphere	biography	phosphorous	hemisphere
atmosphere	diphtheria	symphony	saxophone
sphinx	philosopher	apostrophe	triumphant
asphalt	typhoid	catastrophe	xylophone

Exercise

Use these phrases in sentences.

a clever physician	fine physique
collecting autographs	a touching epitaph
camphorated oil	most emphatic
a graphic account	prophetic warning
sulphurous fumes	the aged philosopher

100 Words That Are Often Mis-Spelt

(a)
also	limit	diary	purpose
already	omit	diamond	pursuit
although	permit	giant	surprise
altogether	welcome	definite	murmur
always	welfare	quite	curtain

(b)
hymn	biscuit	answer	depth
column	county	*enquire	length
condemn	country	forehead	width
solemn	christen	perhaps	conscious
chimney	buried	poultry	excitement

(c)
Arctic	fulfil	all right	convalescent
atrocity	Saturday	quiet	discipline
certainly	scythe	recognise	February
journey	tongue	shepherd	menagerie
obliged	truly	sincerely	reservoir

(d)
fatigue	anxious	benefited	dependants
foreigner	aerial	developed	government
forfeit	genuine	profited	independent
rhubarb	guardian	lightning	mistletoe
subtle	leisure	privilege	Parliament

(e)
calendar	ecstasy	celluloid	carburettor
separate	mosquito	colander	conscientious
exquisite	pamphlet	glycerine	extravagance
lieutenant	queue	harassed	bronchitis
mysterious	schedule	Wednesday	rheumatism

* This word may also be spelt 'inquire'. Likewise 'enquiry' can be spelt 'inquiry'.

100 Words That Are Apt To Be Confused

Write out the meaning of these words and use them in sentences.
Do not attempt to learn them in pairs. Their spelling should be learned only when they are in sentences. The more examples you can give the better you will learn them.

advice	accept	altar	as	beach
advise	except	alter	has	beech
bean	bare	board	borough	brake
been	bear	bored	burrow	break
buy	coarse	council	currant	die
by	course	counsel	current	dye
dear	effect	ear	to	
deer	affect	hear	too	
		here	two	
fined	foul	gamble	groan	heal
find	fowl	gambol	grown	heel
hole	is	leak	lead (metal)	medal
whole	his	leek	led	meddle
muscle	of (ov)	new	pain	pair
mussel	off (off)	knew	pane	pear
peace	peal	practice	principal	right
piece	peel	practise	principle	write
sail	sell	seller	scent	sight
sale	cell	cellar	sent	site
tail	their	tire	were	who's
tale	there	tyre	where	whose

General Revision Tests

(a)	(b)	(c)	(d)
reins	robberies	league	development
fetch	funeral	amusing	successful
mental	chisel	attic	present
accident	daffodil	doubtful	David's hands
message	weight	cellar	sandwich
peaceful	puzzle	wrinkle	penknives
trigger	quarrel	excitement	sensible
barrel	scissors	neighbour	singeing
daughter	permission	devoured	wrench
pennies	grammar	developed	axle

(e)	(f)	(g)	(h)
satchel	complexion	foreigner	necessity
oases	beautiful	aggravate	discipline
scullery	battalion	calendar	restaurant
paraffin	allotment	serviceable	embarrassed
visitor	apologies	accelerate	exaggerate
pianos	opportunity	extinguishes	harassed
nuisance	description	illustration	diphtheria
wriggle	tobacco	its paw	carburettor
bicycle	cauliflower	disqualified	rheumatism
theatre	discusses	abscess	celluloid